The World That Don Built

by Harry P Materne

For our loves

The World That Don Built

By

Harry P Materne, III

Artwork by Karleen Materne

ISBN 978-1-716-89598-2

Forward

It was a sunny Valentine's Day afternoon in February. I had returned home after an emotionally exhausting week at school, as one of my friends and coworkers had died. It was particularly difficult because this coworker had such an amazing relationship with my students and the community. Darryl was one of our bus drivers and in just ten minutes per day, he changed lives. He changed lives and for the better. Every day.

These were the facts I was lamenting that sunny Valentine's Day: how one man in such a small capacity could change the world daily while so many others with money, power and influence chose to do little or worse—create division and hate between people. Thinking back, I don't think there's ever been a time in my adult life where I could remember so many people who were as consistently angry and divided as they are now. And I thought, "Well, this is the world that Trump built."

It was at that moment on that sunny Valentine's Day afternoon that I paused. An idea took hold. I walked into the kitchen and told my husband Harry that he was going to write a book. He looked at me as if I were crazy so I asked, "You know the kid's book, *The House That Jack Built*?" He nodded. I replied, "Well, you're going to write *The World That Don Built*."

And he did.

In an hour.

When Harry finished he said, "It may not come to anything, but I feel better." That evening we laughed and tossed out ideas as to how I should illustrate it. It was a great night.

And then, like the thief in the night one only hears about, the unimaginable happened. Harry died suddenly and unexpectedly the next morning. Several hours later I vowed I would illustrate and publish his book. I did and **this** is 'that' book. To quote my husband, "It may not come to anything, but I feel better."

Karleen Materne

This is the world that Don built.

This is the con

That lay at the base

Of the world that Don built.

These are the dupes

Who believed in the con

That lay at the base

Of the world that Don built.

These are the facts

That exposed the dupes

Who believed in the con

That lay at the base

Of the world that Don built.

This is the FOX with the loud bullhorn

That tossed the facts

That exposed the dupes

That believed in the con

That lay at the base

Of the world that Don built.

The
Broadcasting
Bunch

This is the media somewhat forlorn

Who challenged the FOX with the loud bullhorn

That tossed the facts

That exposed the dupes

That believed in the con

That lay at the base

Of the world that Don built.

This is the document aged and worn

That bolstered the media somewhat forlorn

Who challenged the FOX with the loud bullhorn

That tossed the facts

That exposed the dupes

That believed in the con

That lay at the base

Of the world that Don built.

This is the spotlight that shown in the morn

That shined on the document aged and worn

That bolstered the media somewhat forlorn

Who challenged the FOX with the loud bullhorn

That tossed the facts

That exposed the dupes

That believed in the con

That lay at the base

Of the world that Don built.

These are the people so filled with scorn

Who saw the light that shown in the morn

That bolstered the media somewhat forlorn

Who challenged the FOX with the loud bullhorn

That tossed the facts

That exposed the dupes

That believed in the con

That lay at the base

Of the world that Don built.

These are the voters who'll channel that scorn

And filled with that light will vote to be shorn

Of the man who trampled the document

Aged and worn

And railed at the media somewhat forlorn

That challenged the FOX with the loud bullhorn

The facts are facts.

The dupes are dupes.

Don't believe in the con

That lies at the base

Of the world that Don built.

About the Author

Harry P Materne (1956-2020) was born in St. Louis, Missouri to a department store clerk and WWII Veteran. The Materne's lived in St. Louis until 1963 when his father started working for Wright Patterson Air Force Base in Dayton, OH.

Harry graduated with honors from Meadowview High School and immediately joined the Army. He was stationed in Berlin during The Cold War where he was a proud member of The Berlin Brigade. It was there that he performed military intelligence as an interpreter/translator. Harry's plan to remain in the military after his four year stint was scrapped when, in 1981, a life altering car crash caused him to change his career path.

Harry went on to earn his degree in German and English Education from Wright State University. He taught at Stebbins High school in Riverside. In 1990 a new teacher captured his heart and made all of his days brighter. They were married for 28 years and have two amazing children.

The World That Don Built is Harry's only written work. A portion of the proceeds from the sale of this book go to the Harry P Materne Scholarship Fund for Aspiring Writers.

Harry's ashes are interred at the Dayton National Cemetery in Ohio.